Step Away From the Kitten

Ali Sparkes

Illustrated by Louis Roskosch

OXFORD
UNIVERSITY PRESS

Contents

Man's Best Friend 6
Safety in the Skies...12
Pigeon Post 16
Who's Yellow? 20
Lifesavers Who Really Mean It 22
Big Pals 24
The Ever-Helpful Horse 28
Bullet Ants: The Good, the Bad and the Puffy 30
Magical Maggoty Mates 32
Space Monkeys, Rocket Dogs and Ant-ronauts..................34
Glossary 38
Index 39

Look. There's nothing wrong with a kitten.

It's cute. It's cuddly. It mews.
But does it really help you in a crisis?
Well, ask yourself this: would this kitten …

Save you from a collapsed building?

Remove a nasty infection?

Stitch up a wound?

Warn you of poisonous gas?

Contact your **allies** in a war zone?

No. It wouldn't.

Let's just check out its score ...

Pet Score Card

Kitten
Cuteness: 10/10
Effort to look after: 6/10
Usefulness: 1/10

If you must get a pet, there are some much more useful options.

All kinds of animals help us out on a daily basis. Some of them need a bit of training. Some of them do it just because they want to. Others aren't even aware of how incredibly useful they are. But *you* can find out with this guide to handy, helpful creatures who can improve your life ... or even save it.

What is your emergency?

My house has just collapsed! I'm trapped under a wardrobe!

Don't panic. A **Labrador** is on its way.

What? I need help, not walkies!

Man's Best Friend

She's only three years old, but she's already trained to sniff out people buried in **rubble**. She can help out in earthquake zones or in houses which have collapsed in fires or explosions.

This is Amber. She's a search and rescue dog with the Buckinghamshire Fire and Rescue Service in the United Kingdom. Check out the funky red dog shoes! These are specially designed for dogs who do the kind of job that Amber does. While she's searching through rubble, she could tread on glass, sharp metal or areas that are still hot or burning.

Amber's training has been intense and thorough, and her Fire and Rescue handler trained alongside her. Human and dog must both stay fit and healthy. They are a team. They play together too because play is important to keep a Fire and Rescue dog happy and alert.

Some dogs are quite specialized in their kinds of rescue. Here's one.

This retriever works with an avalanche rescue team in Canada and sniffs out people who have been buried in snow. All this is possible because of the extraordinary superpower that dogs have. Guess what it is!

Yes, a dog's nose is its superpower.

Depending on the **breed**, a dog's sense of smell is at least 1000 times more sensitive than a human's. This is because dogs use smells to understand the world around them. They get most of their information through their noses – unlike humans, who use other senses like sight and touch.

A dog's nose is usually **moist** and this helps it to smell. Scent **molecules** are captured by the wet **mucus** inside its nose. A dog will often wet its nose with its tongue – which may be why dogs' tongues are so long!

Pet Score Card

Rescue Dog
Cuteness: 9/10
Effort to look after: 8/10
Usefulness: 10/10

PRESCRIPTION

Two hours of dog therapy.

Take twice a week.

Let's make friends with Lucy.

Lucy's job is just to be ... lovely, sweet, calm, Lucy. She is a **therapy** dog.

She is brought into the children's ward, and other wards all around the hospital, to cheer people up. Therapy dogs must be friendly, affectionate and calm. They must be kept very clean and neat and be good with all kinds of people, noises and smells.

Scientific studies have shown that cuddling and stroking a dog is good for your health. And of course, going out for walks with a dog helps your health and fitness too. Basically, spending time with a good doggy just makes us feel better.

Pet Score Card

Therapy Dog

Cuteness: 9/10

Effort to look after: 7/10

Usefulness: 8/10

Safety in the Skies

"This is your captain speaking. Please fasten your seat belts for take-off."

Up, up and away you go! Relaaaaaax. Don't worry about that dark grey blur streaking across the flight path on a collision course for disaster ...

Wallop!

The airport-dwelling pigeon is whacked sideways – by Hector the Harris hawk.

Hector has just swooped down from above and stopped that pigeon from hitting your plane's engine, which would have caused big problems. The pigeon is now spinning down to earth, while Hector has saved the lives of a whole planeload of passengers and crew, and they'll never know it.

Hector is one of a team of **raptors** sent out to patrol the airport. There are Harris hawks working at airports all around the world. These large American birds of prey are used to keep other birds away from the planes.

Other raptors are also used in this way. The peregrine falcon can hunt at speeds of over 322 kilometres per hour – and pigeon is usually on its menu.

But the raptors who guard airports don't actually need to catch anything. It's all about fear. If a big, terrifying predator like a Harris hawk shows up at an airport just once a week, pigeons get the message. They may be bird-brained, but they're not stupid.

They go and hang around somewhere else.

Pet Score Card

Harrier Hawk

Cuteness: 3/10

Effort to look after: 9/10

Usefulness: 8/10

But let's not be too hard on the humble pigeon. After all, they've helped to win wars! Pigeons were a vital form of communication during World War I and World War II. Read on …

Pigeon Post

Homing pigeons are amazing **navigators** and people have used them for centuries. In ancient times, the Egyptians and Romans used pigeons to deliver messages during battles.

Carrier pigeons will only go one way: home. So thousands of them were reared in or near military bases and then taken away to war. During World War I, the British Army had a unit especially for these birds called 'The Carrier Pigeon Service'. More than 100 000 pigeons were sent across battlefields and **occupied territory** carrying urgent information. Amazingly, 95 per cent of them got through!

One of the most famous carrier pigeons was Cher Ami. In October 1918, not long before the end of World War I, things were looking very bad for a unit of American soldiers. 194 of them were trapped behind enemy lines, and they had no working radios. What they did have, though, was Cher Ami.

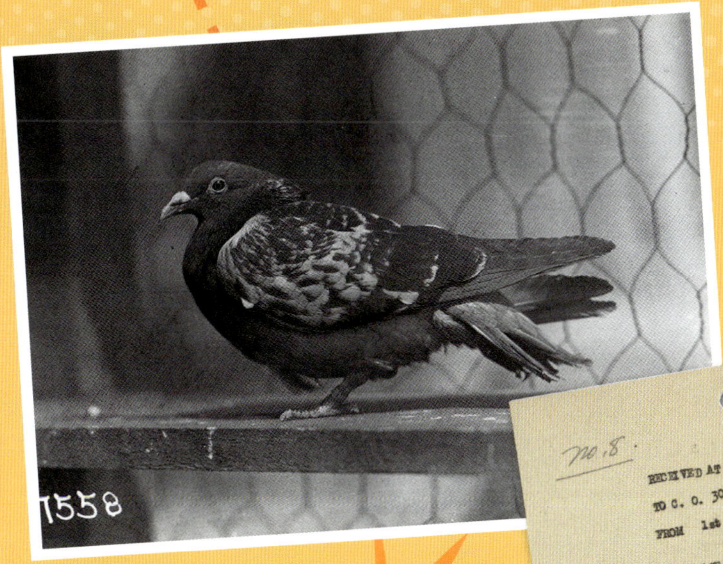

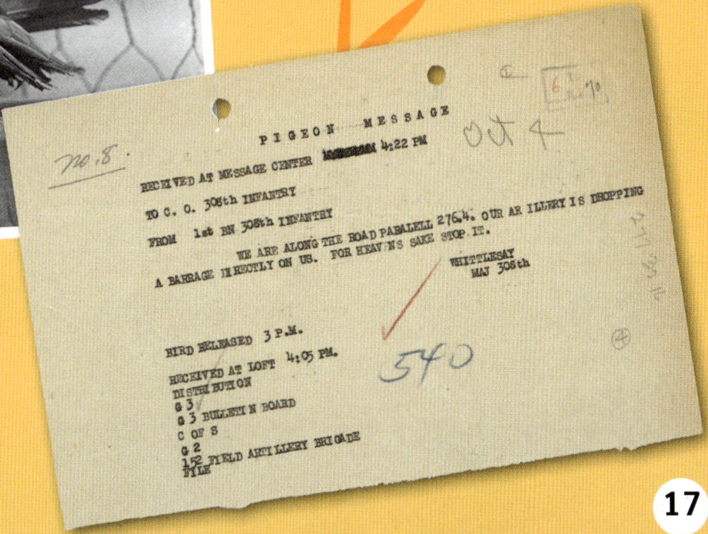

Cher Ami was released and flew the 40 kilometres to the US headquarters in just 25 minutes, carrying the **co-ordinates** of the lost unit's location on her leg. On the way, she was hit in the chest by German gunfire ... but flew on regardless. The Americans successfully rescued all 194 men and Cher Ami was given a medal.

Here's one of the tiny tubes which were attached to carrier pigeons' legs during their wartime service. The paper messages inside were incredibly light and even **microfilm** could be transported like this.

This one is a capsule used during World War II.

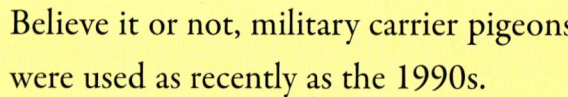

Believe it or not, military carrier pigeons were used as recently as the 1990s.

Pet Score Card

Carrier Pigeon

Cuteness:	3/10
Effort to look after:	6/10
Usefulness:	9/10

Nowadays, we have technology which gives us instant communication anywhere in the world. But what if someone pulls the plug on the power? Better keep a few carrier pigeons on standby just in case!

Who's Yellow?

The colour yellow usually represents cowardice. But for some little feathery friends, being yellow meant being a lifesaver.

Coal mining has always been a dangerous business. As well as underground pit falls and flooding, miners had to cope with dangerous gases which could build up around them. In the early 20th century, their early warning system was ... a canary.

These little yellow finches are very sensitive to **carbon monoxide**. Miners would go down into the pit with a canary in a cage for company – then wait for it to freak out.

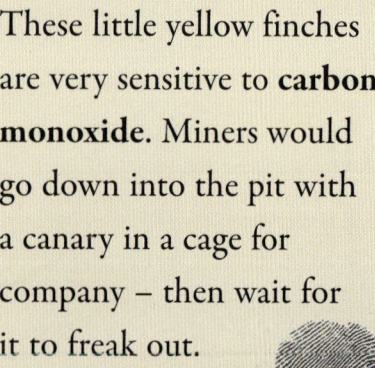

If the canaries started showing signs of distress – or just died – the miners would return to the surface fast. The dangerous gas cannot be smelled by humans, so the yellow canary was quite literally a life saver.

Tweety! What's up?

Pet Score Card

Canary
Cuteness: 7/10
Effort to look after: 5/10
Usefulness: 9/10

In 1986, canaries in British mines were replaced with hand-held digital detectors.

Lifesavers Who Really Mean It

So ... would most of these clever animals help us out if we didn't ask? Dolphins might. Stories of dolphins saving sailors have been told for centuries.

New Zealand, 2004

Dolphins surround swimmers to protect them against great white shark!

The Red Sea, 1996

Dolphins protect shark-bitten swimmer!
Injured British man circled by three bottlenose dolphins.

Italy, 2000

Drowning boy helped back to shore by dolphin!

Dolphins have human-like habits. They live in groups called pods and keep their young close for a year. They've been known to save other species, like whales, by herding them away from dangerously shallow waters.

Pet Score Card

Dolphin
Cuteness: 8/10
Effort to look after: 9/10
Usefulness: 9/10

So if you live on the coast, why not train a dolphin to guard you at all times?

Big Pals

As well as carrying people on their backs for around 4000 years, Asian elephants have been trained to help with farming and **logging**. They have carried soldiers and weapons into war zones and kings and queens on triumphant marches.

But do elephants care about us the way we think dolphins do?

On 26th December 2004, working elephants started to make their own decisions. Many of them were in the tourist trade, giving rides to holidaymakers along the coasts of Indonesia, Sri Lanka, India and Thailand. For no reason, it seemed, they began to cry and trumpet. Those that were **tethered** shook off their chains. Then they headed inland, many of them still carrying their passengers. Their baffled owners followed, trying and failing to get them to turn around.

Within the next hour, a devastating **tsunami** hit the coastline, killing hundreds of thousands of people in eight countries.

There were many stories of people whose lives were saved by elephants. It seemed a large number of people had been taken inland, whether they wanted to go or not. In some cases, the elephants finally stopped just metres away from the reach of the tidal wave.

It's believed that elephants and other animals are more sensitive to the vibrations of the earth. When an earthquake occurred out in the Indian Ocean, sending the tsunami towards the land, the elephants could sense it.

A bit like the canaries in the mineshaft – but a lot bigger.

Did those elephants really deliberately save human lives? Or were they just acting on instinct? In getting away from the incoming tidal wave, were they just taking human passengers with them by chance?

In the days that followed, they helped save more lives by searching through the rubble with their sensitive trunks, sniffing out survivors and helping rescue teams to lift heavy objects.

Pet Score Card

Asian Elephant
Cuteness: 7/10
Effort to look after: 9/10
Usefulness: 10/10

The Ever-Helpful Horse

For thousands of years, horses have been as helpful to humans as dogs, even in the midst of terrifying war zones.

Millions of horses died on both sides in World War I. Afterwards, the way horses were used within the army changed. Today, the British Household Cavalry Mounted Regiment continues to train its soldiers to work with horses, but mostly for parades, where they act as a bodyguard for the **monarch**.

Horses also play an important role in today's police forces. They are chosen for their intelligence and **stability** and are trained for six months before going to work.

When they are on duty in crowded situations, horses wear protective shin pads around their legs. They also have visors across their faces, just like the officers riding them.

Because they don't panic when they hear loud noises, these horses are used at important public occasions and as a calming presence at sporting events.

One mounted police officer = 12 officers on foot

Pet Score Card

Horse
Cuteness: 8/10
Effort to look after: 8/10
Usefulness: 8/10

Bullet Ants: The Good, the Bad and the Puffy

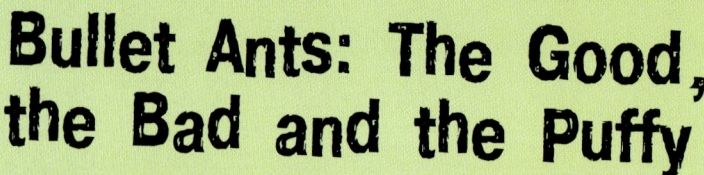

Imagine you're stranded in the Nicaraguan jungle with a nasty cut on your leg. Then you spot a line of ants trekking past you.

Bad news. These are bullet ants. Their sting is about 30 times more painful than a wasp sting. There's a **neurotoxin** in their venom which causes shaking, **paralysis** and even death. Yikes!

Good news! Those bullet ants could solve your open wound problem. Local tribespeople in Paraguay and Nicaragua use the jaws of bullet ants to stitch up wounds.

How to save your life with an ant

1. Hold edges of wound together.

2. Position head of bullet ant above wound.

3. Allow angry ant to bite flesh.

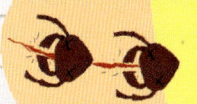

4. Twist ant to snap head off, leaving jaws stapling flesh together.

5. Repeat as needed.

6. Note: ant's saliva will cause flesh to swell, sealing wound tightly.

So ... they're quite useful, after all! That's as long as you don't mind a bite which would make even the toughest kid in school cry ...

Pet Score Card

Bullet Ants
Cuteness: 1/10
Effort to look after: 8/10
Usefulness: 7/10

Magical Maggoty Mates

OK ... so maybe bullet ants are a little bit risky to keep as a pet.

But maggots ... now they are brilliantly useful for tackling wounds, and they don't sting at all! Maggots eat dead **tissue** and leave healthy tissue clean and uninfected. Scientists have discovered something magical about maggot slime. It controls **inflammation** like a natural disinfectant.

Back in the 18th century, physicians in Napoleon Bonaparte's army used maggots to clean wounds on soldiers. During World War I, soldiers with maggots in their wounds seemed to recover more quickly than those without maggots, and they had less swelling and infection too.

When **penicillin** was discovered, maggot therapy was largely forgotten. But now, because penicillin is becoming less effective against some infections, the maggot is back! Hospitals are once again introducing maggots to their patients' wounds and seeing brilliant results.

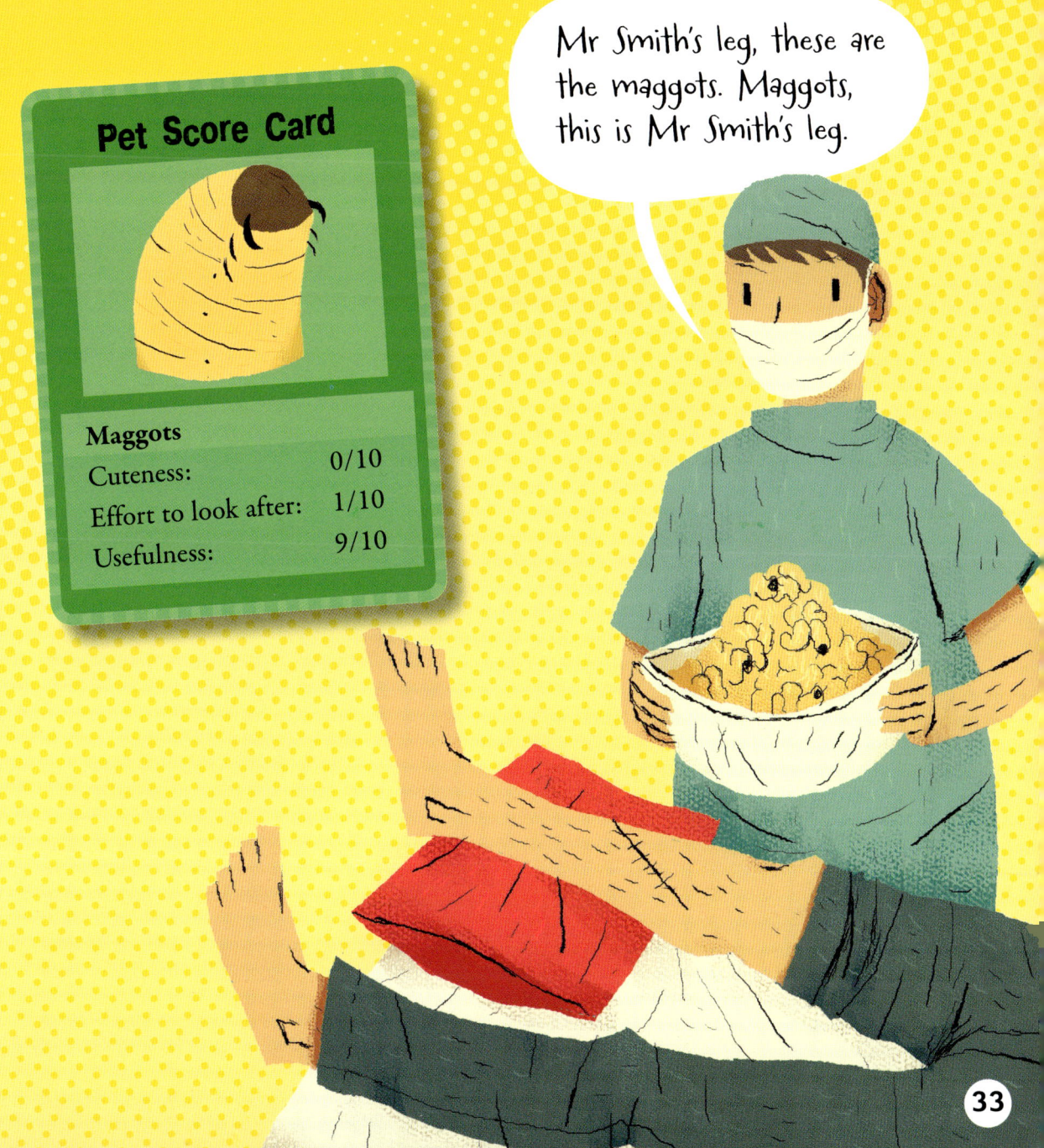

Space Monkeys, Rocket Dogs and Ant-ronauts

Patricia and Mike, along with Mildred and Albert, didn't know it, but they were about to make history. On 22nd May 1952, the two couples boarded the Aerobee at an air force base in New Mexico and took a short flight of just 36 miles ...

upwards ...
at 3200 kilometres per hour ...

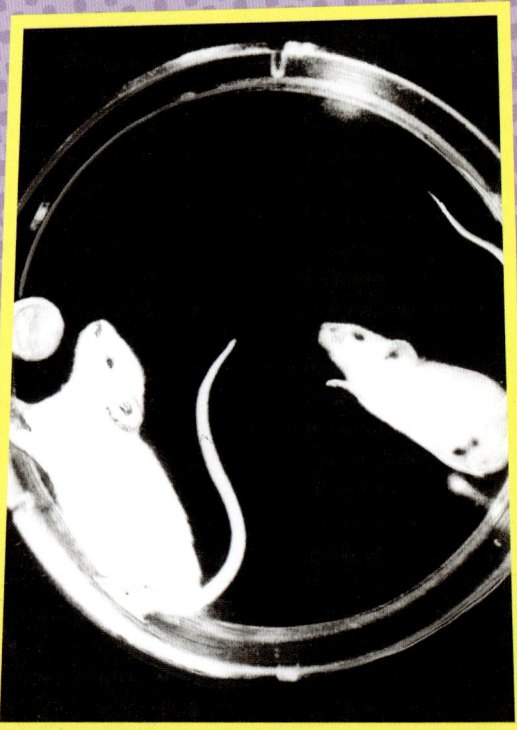

Patricia and Mike were Philippine monkeys and Mildred and Albert were white mice. Although Patricia and Mike were strapped in during the journey, Mildred and Albert were in a slowly rotating drum. The drum enabled them to experience weightlessness during their trip.

What makes this really amazing is that all of them made it back alive.

Other animal helpers for the space programme didn't come out of it so well. The first monkeys sent into space in 1948 and 1949 did not survive the impact when the V-2 Blossom spacecraft returned to Earth with a considerable thud.

Oh, and the first mouse to go up in a V-2 in 1950 didn't make it back squeaking, either.

In fact, throughout the 1950s and 1960s, the United States of America and the Soviet Union put monkeys, chimps, dogs, mice, rabbits, spiders, stick insects, fish, ants, cats, jellyfish, amoebas and algae into orbit. All the **data** recorded from these experiments helped scientists understand how human astronauts would manage in space. Without them, we would never have got a man on the moon.

Well, that about wraps it up for the human race's most useful pets.

Oh, hold on! Did you see what I saw in that list of space pets?

... monkeys, chimps, dogs, mice, rabbits, spiders, stick insects, fish, ants, cats, jellyfish, amoebas and algae ...

Cats.

Cats! Grown up kittens! Really?

It's true!

On 18th October 1963, French scientists sent the first cat into space on a Veronique V47 rocket. The cat, named Félicette, survived the return to Earth.

Maybe you don't have to step away from the kitten after all – especially if you're planning to test a spaceship.

But that would be mean. Look at him! Aaaaw, poor cute little kitty-witty-woo!

Oh, go on then ... hand him over for a cuddle.

Glossary

allies: a group of countries that help each other during wartime

breed: animals of a specific type which all have certain characteristics

carbon monoxide: a poisonous gas which has no colour or smell to humans

co-ordinates: numbers which tell you where something is on a map

data: information collected for reference

inflammation: condition that causes flesh to become hot, red, swollen and sore because of injury or infection

logging: cutting down trees for their wood to be sold

Labrador: a medium-sized breed of dog with a short yellow or brown coat

microfilm: film on which documents are photographed at reduced size

moist: slightly wet

molecules: very tiny pieces of something

monarch: a ruler such as a king or queen

mucus: a slimy substance that protects certain parts of the body, such as the nose

navigators: people or animals who know where they are and can plan a route

neurotoxin: a poison that affects the body's nervous system

occupied territory: land taken over by an enemy

paralysis: being unable to move

penicillin: an antibiotic, or medicine, used to treat illnesses or diseases

raptors: birds of prey, who hunt other animals for food

rubble: debris from destroyed buildings such as brick, stone and concrete

stability: being calm and secure, not easily disturbed

tethered: tied up with a rope or chain

tissue: cells that make up skin, organs and muscles inside the body

tsunami: a very high, large wave in the ocean caused by an earthquake under the sea

therapy: treatment to heal injury or ease pain

Index

ants 30–31
cats 36–37
dolphins 22–23
elephants 24–27
health 10–11, 30–31, 32–33
horses 28–29
insects 30–33, 36
maggots 32–33
mice 34–36
monkeys 34–36
rescue 6–8, 22–23, 24–27, 17–18
scientists 32, 36
space travel 34–37
messages 16–19
smell 8–9, 21
soldiers 16–18, 32
kittens 4–5, 37
dogs 6–11
hospitals 10–11, 33
training 7, 28
Pet Score Cards 5, 9, 11, 15, 19, 21, 23, 27, 29, 31, 33
birds 12–21

About the Author

I love dogs and cats, but I am horribly allergic to them. I'm fine with maggots but find it hard to bond with them as pets. They're very hard to take for a walk. My adventure stories (the Shapeshifter and SWITCH series) feature a lot of wildlife, from foxes and falcons to crane flies (daddy-long-legs) and Great Diving Beetles – and I am amazed at how weird and wonderful the facts about these creatures are. My favourite fact is that scorpions can be frozen solid, and then just walk away when defrosted!

Greg Foot, Series Editor

I've loved science ever since the day I took my papier mâché volcano into school. I filled it with far too much baking powder, vinegar and red food colouring, and WHOOSH! I covered the classroom ceiling in red goo. Now I've got the best job in the world: I present TV shows for the BBC, answer kids' science questions on YouTube, and make huge explosions on stage at festivals!

Working on TreeTops inFact has been great fun. There are so many brilliant books, and guess what ... they're all packed full of awesome facts! What's your favourite?